W9-BEV-331

WITHDRAWN

Profiles of the Presidents

CHESTER A. ARTHUR

★ ★ ★

Profiles of the Presidents

CHESTER A. ARTHUR

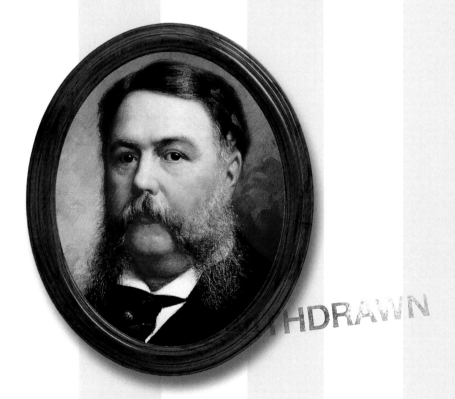

by Andrew Santella

Content Adviser: John P. Dumville, Historic Sites Operations Chief, Vermont Division for Historic Preservation, Montpelier, Vermont

Reading Adviser: Dr. Linda D. Labbo, Department of Reading Education, College of Education, The University of Georgia

COMPASS POINT BOOKS MINNEAPOLIS, MINNESOTA

Compass Point Books
3109 West 50th Street, #115
Minneapolis, MN 55410

Visit Compass Point Books on the Internet at *www.compasspointbooks.com*
or e-mail your request to *custserv@compasspointbooks.com*

Photographs ©: Bettmann/Corbis, cover, 3, 15, 35; North Wind Picture Archives, 6, 8, 10 (bottom), 11, 16, 20, 23, 25, 33, 34, 37, 38, 46, 58 (top left), 59 (top left); Lombard Antiquarian Maps & Prints, 7; George Wuerthner, 9, 54 (left); Library of Congress, 10 (top), 21, 22, 24, 27, 55 (middle right), 56 (left), 57 (left, all); Special Collections of Schaffer Library, Union College, Schenectady, New York, 12, 55 (top left); Hulton Archive/by Getty Images, 13, 30, 31, 39, 40, 41, 49, 55 (top & bottom right), 56 (top right), 58 (right), 59 (right, all); National Portrait Gallery, Smithsonian Institution/Art Resource, N.Y., 14 (top), 26; Special Collections Department, University of Virginia Library, 14 (bottom), 55 (bottom left); Corbis, 17, 19, 28, 32, 47; Jeffrey Kraus Photographic Antiques, 18; Naval Historical Center, 43; White House Historical Association, FBJ Collection, Library of Congress, (984), 44, 58 (bottom left); White House Historical Association, White House Collection, (135), 45; 1998, ChrisTina Leimer, The Tombstone Traveller's Guide, 50, 59 (bottom left); Texas State Library & Archives Commission, 54 (top right); Bruce Burkhardt/Corbis, 54 (bottom right); Union Pacific Museum Collection, 56 (bottom right); Denver Public Library, Western History Collection, 57 (right).

Editors: E. Russell Primm, Emily J. Dolbear, Melissa McDaniel, and Catherine Neitge
Photo Researcher: Svetlana Zhurkina
Photo Selector: Linda S. Koutris
Designer: The Design Lab
Cartographer: XNR Productions, Inc.

Library of Congress Cataloging-in-Publication Data
Santella, Andrew.
  Chester A. Arthur / by Andrew Santella.
    p. cm. — (Profiles of the presidents)
 Summary: A biography of the twenty-first president of the United States, discussing his personal life, education, and political career.
 Includes bibliographical references and index.
  ISBN 0-7565-0268-3 (hardcover : alk. paper)
  1. Arthur, Chester Alan, 1829–1886—Juvenile literature. 2. Presidents—United States—Biography—Juvenile literature. [1. Arthur, Chester Alan, 1829–1886. 2. Presidents.] I. Title. II. Series.
  E692 .S26 2003
  973.8'4'092—dc21   2002153302

Table of Contents

★ ★ ★

*NOTE: In this book, words that are defined in the glossary are
in **bold** the first time they appear in the text.*

The Unknown President

★ ★ ★

The news shocked the nation. On July 2, 1881, President James A. Garfield was shot while walking across a Washington, D.C., train station. Garfield survived, but his wounds left him near death. Doctors discovered that one bullet had

The shooting of ▾ James A. Garfield in July 1881

lodged very near Garfield's spine. They feared that if they tried to remove the bullet, they might accidentally kill the president. There was little they could do but hope he would recover from his wounds.

For two months, Garfield's condition remained serious. As it became clear that he might not survive, people looked to the man who would replace him. When a president dies in office, the vice president takes his place. In 1881, the idea of Vice President Chester A. Arthur taking on the highest office in the country worried many people. Until he became vice president, Arthur was not well known as a politician and had never been elected to office. Even after he became vice president, Americans did not know much about him. Then, in the tense times following Garfield's shooting, they learned some troubling things about him.

Arthur did not get along with President Garfield. As vice president, he remained friends with some of the most **corrupt** politicians in the United States. Not surprisingly,

▲ *Americans were concerned about Chester A. Arthur taking on the responsibilities of the presidency in 1881.*

the thought of Arthur living in the White House frightened many Americans. One senator went so far as to offer a prayer that Arthur would never become president.

On September 19, 1881, President Garfield died of the wounds he had suffered ten weeks earlier. When Arthur learned of the president's death, he put his head in his hands and cried. Early the next morning, Chester A. Arthur was sworn in as president of the United States. The nation waited anxiously to learn what sort of president he would be.

James Garfield's coffin on display for the public to view in Washington, D.C., in September 1881

Early Years

★ ★ ★

Chester Alan Arthur was born on October 5, 1829, in Fairfield, Vermont. He was the fifth child and the first son born to William and Malvina Arthur. William Arthur had always hoped for at least one son. When Malvina gave birth to Chester, William was overjoyed.

William Arthur had moved to the United States from northern Ireland. He became a minister at a Baptist church in Fairfield, a farming community of 2,200 people. The Arthurs lived in a simple cabin there. William Arthur was not a popular man in Fairfield. He was a strong and forceful abolition- ist, which is a person who wanted to outlaw slavery everywhere in the United

▼ A replica of the Arthur home in Fairfield, Vermont

States. At that time, slavery was allowed in the Southern states but was banned in the Northern states. During the 1830s, few members of Arthur's church were ready to support abolition. Arthur often had disagreements with them over the issue of slavery.

The Reverend ▾
William Arthur

Finally, those disagreements drove the Arthurs out of Fairfield. Over the next ten years, William Arthur kept moving his family and looking for a church where he would be welcomed as a minister. The Arthurs moved five times during the 1830s.

In 1839, the family moved to Union Village, New York, just across

A view of ▸
Schenectady, New
York, home of
Union College

the border from Vermont. There, young Chester attended school for the first time. Until then, his mother had taught him at home. By the time Chester was fourteen, he was beginning to make plans to attend college.

In 1844, the family moved again to nearby Greenwich, New York. William Arthur became a minister at the First Baptist Church there, and Chester started taking classes at a local school called the Lyceum. The Lyceum offered classes that prepared young men to attend nearby Union College. While attending the Lyceum, Chester received his first education in politics, as well. He joined a group of students supporting Kentucky's Henry Clay in the 1844 presidential election. Chester took part in a **brawl** with some people who supported another **candidate.** For Chester, it was the first of many political battles to come.

▼ *Henry Clay ran for president in 1844.*

Chester began attending Union College in the fall of 1845, just before his sixteenth birthday. He had received such a good education at the Lyceum that he was able to skip one year of college. At Union College, however, Chester sometimes seemed more interested in his social life than in his studies. Still, his grades placed him near the top of his class, and he was elected to Phi Beta Kappa, a national honor society. When he graduated in 1848, he was asked to give a speech at the ceremony.

Union College in Schenectady, New York, in the mid 1800s ▾

The Law and a Divided Nation

★ ★ ★

Chester Arthur had big plans for his life after college. He would study law, become a lawyer, and move to New York City. First, however, he had to make enough money to pay

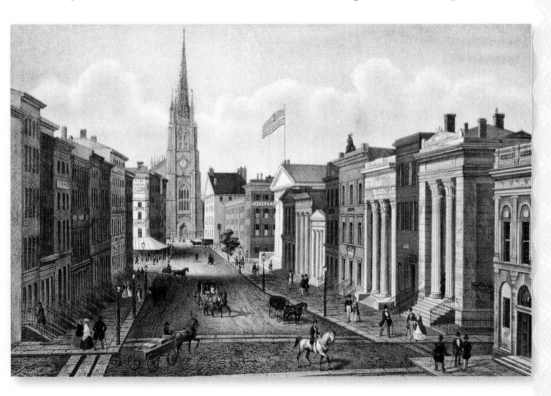

▼ *A view of New York City's Wall Street in 1847*

Arthur during his
years as a lawyer
in New York

An article from
the Staunton
Spectator *summa-
rizing the Lemmon
slave case in 1860*

THE LEMMON SLAVE CASE.—Several years
ago, a Mrs. Lemmon, of Virginia, went to New
York with her family, to take passage for Texas,
where she proposed to settle. Her slaves were
liberated in New York city, on the ground that
the local laws prohibited slavery. This gave
rise to a suit at law, which has recently been
decided by the New York Court of Appeals.—
The opinion of the Court, delivered by Judge
Denio, holds that when Mrs. Lemmon carried
her slaves to New York she did not carry there
the laws of Virginia. Her claim to hold them
rested on the ground that, as a citizen of the
United States, she was entitled, under the Con-
stitution, to all the privileges that she had in
Virginia. Judge D. denies this, and affirms that
the "privileges and immunities" to which a Vir-
ginian is entitled in New York are not those of
a citizen of Virginia, but those of a citizen of
New York. And the right to hold slaves, he
says, is not one of the privileges and immunities
of citizens of New York. Three of the Judges
—Comstock, Seden and Clark—dissent from the
judgement pronounced in this case; and five—
Denio, Davis, Wright, Bacon and Welles—con-
cur therein.

for his education as a lawyer. For
five years, he taught school in
small towns in New York and
Vermont. In the evenings and
on weekends, he studied law.

In 1853, he gave up teach-
ing and moved to New York
City. There he landed a job as
a clerk in the law office of E. D.
Culver. The following year, he
passed the exam to become a
lawyer in New York. He joined
Culver's law practice, which
was renamed Culver, Parker
and Arthur.

Almost immediately,
young Chester Arthur
became involved in two
high-profile cases. Both
involved the rights of
African-Americans in
New York. In the Lem-
mon slave case, Arthur's

law firm helped win freedom for eight slaves who had been brought to New York in 1852 by a Virginia slave owner named Jonathan Lemmon. Abolitionists argued that Lemmon's slaves should be freed because New York state laws banned slavery. Lemmon's lawyers replied that New York's slavery laws did not apply to slave owners who didn't live in New York. Between 1856 and 1860, New York courts ruled that Lemmon did not have the right to keep slaves in New York.

In 1854, Arthur represented a free African-American schoolteacher named Elizabeth Jennings in her lawsuit against a New York City streetcar company. At that time,

▾ *A horse car in New York in the late 1800s*

New York City streetcars had separate sections for blacks and whites. Earlier that year, Jennings had been forced to leave the whites-only section of a streetcar. In court, Arthur won a $250 judgment against the company. More importantly, the case convinced all New York City transportation companies to allow African-Americans to sit wherever they wanted.

During the 1850s, the conflict between abolitionists and slave owners threatened to tear the nation apart. Nowhere was that conflict more violent than in Kansas

Americans from other states on their way to Kansas Territory during the 1850s to vote on the issue of slavery

Territory. There, people who were for and against slavery fought for control of the government. Hundreds of abolitionists from the Northeast headed for Kansas to fight the spread of slavery. In 1856, Arthur traveled to Kansas with his friend and new law partner Henry Gardiner. They saw for themselves how violent the fight over slavery had become.

Before he left for Kansas, Arthur had become engaged to a woman named Ellen Lewis Herndon. Nicknamed Nell, Herndon was the daughter of a well-known explorer and sea captain named William Herndon. While Arthur was in Kansas, he received a letter from Nell. Her father had died in a shipwreck off the coast of North Carolina, and she needed Arthur's help. Arthur rushed home to comfort her. He helped Nell and her mother with their legal and financial business. On October 25, 1859, Chester Arthur and Nell Herndon were married in New York City.

▲ *Ellen Lewis Herndon married Chester Arthur in 1859.*

The Spoils System

★ ★ ★

Arthur began his married life with Nell in New York and was determined to make a success of himself. One of the best places for a young lawyer to make his mark was in politics. In 1860, Arthur began working for a powerful New York politician named Thurlow Weed.

In the mid-1800s, political parties sometimes used questionable methods to get power. Weed was a party leader and a master of these methods. Politicians like Weed convinced large numbers of people to work to elect their party's candi-

Thurlow Weed was an important New York politician during the mid-1800s.

dates to local offices. If the party won the election, these workers were rewarded with well-paying government jobs. Sometimes these jobs required little work, yet the people who held them were able to make a good living. In return, workers were expected to give a portion of their salaries back to the party. Party leaders then used that money to elect more candidates, who could offer more jobs to party workers.

▾ *The Department of the Treasury building in the mid-1800s*

Abraham Lincoln ▶ was elected president in 1860.

This style of politics was known as the spoils system. Spoils are what the winner of a war takes from the loser. The spoils system worked so well that local political parties like Weed's became known as machines. Arthur was rewarded for his work in the Weed machine in 1860 when he was given a job in the New York state **militia.**

Then, in 1861, the long-running national conflict over slavery exploded into war. Abraham Lincoln had been elected president. Many Southerners thought he would end slavery. Following his election, eleven Southern states seceded, or broke away, from the Union. Lincoln did not think they had the right to leave the Union. The Civil War (1861–1865) had begun.

With the start of the war, Arthur was given a new job in the office of the quarter-master general. This office was in charge of supplying food, clothing, equipment, and shelter to New York militia troops. Arthur performed so well in his new job that he was promoted in 1862 to the position of quartermaster general, the person in charge of the office.

Arthur soon became known as a promising figure in the New York Republican

▾ *Arthur as the quarter-master general of New York during the Civil War*

Party. In 1868, he was appointed to head the group that ran party business in New York. In this job, he worked with U.S. Senator Roscoe Conkling to make the Republican machine more powerful than ever. Conkling's supporters, who were called Stalwarts, became an important force in national politics. In 1868, Conkling and the Stalwarts helped elect Ulysses S. Grant president of the United States. Grant thanked the Stalwarts by giving many of them government jobs.

One of the best jobs went to Arthur. In 1871, he was made collector of the Port of New York at the New York Custom House. The New York Custom House was a huge office. Thirteen hundred people worked there and collected taxes on goods shipped into the Port of New York.

The spoils system was working well for Arthur. He and Nell were able to move into a large house with many servants. They hired private tutors for their son, Alan. (A son born in 1860 had died when he was only two.) In 1871, Nell gave birth to a daughter named Ellen Herndon Arthur.

◄ *Elegant crowds on New York City's Broadway in the late 1800s*

The spoils system may have helped Arthur, but it often produced wasteful and corrupt government offices. Because workers had been handed their jobs, they sometimes didn't put much effort into their work. Some employees used their jobs to steal money. At the New York Custom House, which Arthur ran, certain workers kept part of the tax money they had collected for the government. During the 1870s, it became clear to more and more people that the spoils system needed to be changed.

*The New York ▼
Custom House*

◄ *President Rutherford B. Hayes tried to end government corruption.*

In 1876, Rutherford B. Hayes was elected president. Hayes vowed to wipe out corruption in government. He took aim at the New York Custom House. Hayes did not accuse Arthur of dishonesty, but he believed that Arthur had not done enough to stop the workers there from being corrupt. In 1878, Arthur was forced out of his job.

The Vice President

★ ★ ★

Arthur remained active in politics, and in 1880 he saw his chance to get back to a position of power. Along with Conkling and other Stalwarts, Arthur worked hard to return Ulysses S. Grant to the White House. The Republican Party, however, threw its support behind Ohio con-

Former Civil War general and president Ulysses S. Grant

gressman James A. Garfield instead of former President Grant. This angered the Stalwarts. Republican Party leaders knew they would need the Stalwarts' support to get Garfield elected, so they offered to make Arthur the vice presidential candidate. They hoped this might convince the Stalwarts to help elect Garfield president.

◄ *A campaign poster from 1880 showing Republican running mates James A. Garfield (left) and Chester A. Arthur*

The plan worked. Arthur was happy to become the Republican candidate for vice president. He **campaigned** in New York and other states to convince people to vote for

Nell Arthur died of ◆
pneumonia in 1880,
the same year her
husband was elected
vice president.

Garfield. He and Garfield were running against Democratic Party candidates Winfield S. Hancock and William H. English. A third candidate, James B. Weaver, ran under the banner of the Greenback-Labor Party. The Republicans won the election with 214 electoral college votes. The Democrats received 155, and Weaver won none.

Arthur was now vice president—just one step away from the highest office in the country. He enjoyed the high status of the vice presidency. Arthur mingled with the rich and powerful, and he dressed in the finest and most fashionable clothes. His charm and good manners earned him the nickname the Gentleman Boss. Nell

Arthur never had the chance to enjoy her husband's new life in Washington, however. In January 1880, she died of **pneumonia** at the age of forty-two.

Some of Arthur's enemies worried that he would bring corruption to the Garfield presidency. They remembered the widespread dishonesty at the New York Custom House under Arthur's leadership. They also knew, though, that Arthur would have little power as vice president. His job was mainly to be ready to step in if something should happen to the president. "It is true General Garfield . . . may die during his term in office, but this is too unlikely," wrote one magazine reporter. No one had any idea how soon that awful possibility would come to pass.

From the start of his term in office, Garfield vowed to end government corruption. He called for government workers to be hired based on their abilities instead of their political connections. Since this would deal a deadly blow to the spoils system that had made Arthur powerful, Arthur resisted these changes. As a result, the president and vice president found themselves disagreeing on the most important political issue of the time. In fact, Arthur was more loyal to his old friend Conkling

President Garfield ▶
did not rely on
Arthur for advice.

than he was to President Garfield. Arthur never became
one of Garfield's trusted advisers.

Everything changed on July 2, 1881, less than four
months into Garfield's presidency. Garfield was making his

way through a railroad station in Washington, D.C., when he was shot several times. The gunman was a disturbed Stalwart named Charles Guiteau. He had worked to help elect Garfield, and had hoped to be rewarded with a government job. When he was refused, he attacked Garfield. Later, as Garfield lay wounded, Guiteau told police that he was a friend of Arthur's. That was not true, but it made some suspect that Arthur was behind the shooting.

▼ Presidential assassin Charles Guiteau in 1881

In fact, Arthur was horrified by the attack. He hoped for Garfield's recovery, and he refused any offer to take power while the president was still alive. On September 19, Arthur learned that Garfield had died. When reporters rushed to speak to Arthur about the news, they were told that he was alone in his room, weeping.

Arthur was sworn ▶
in as president
at his home.

Now Arthur had to step into the presidency. His
friends and his son, Alan, hurried to be by his side.
Messengers were sent to find a judge who would give him
the presidential oath of office. In the middle of the night,
New York Supreme Court Justice John R. Brady came to
Arthur's room. Arthur took the brief oath that made him
the twenty-first president of the United States.

President Arthur

★ ★ ★

One of Arthur's first jobs as president was to fill open positions in his cabinet, the group of department heads who advise the president on important matters. Soon after Garfield's death, three cabinet officials quit, leaving Arthur free to choose new politicians to take their place. Arthur chose a Stalwart named Charles J. Folger to serve as secretary of the treasury. A longtime supporter named Benjamin H. Brewster became attorney general.

Charles J. Folger became secretary of the treasury under Arthur.

Benjamin H. Brewster ▶
was Arthur's choice
for attorney general.

Arthur also had to select a new secretary of state,
the president's top adviser for dealing with foreign
countries. This was the most prized job in the cabinet,
and many people assumed that Arthur would name his
old friend Roscoe Conkling to the job. After all, it was

Conkling who had helped Arthur become a powerful politician. However, Arthur didn't choose Conkling. He was determined to keep his presidency free of machine politics. Arthur instead picked Frederick T. Frelinghuysen, a former senator from New Jersey.

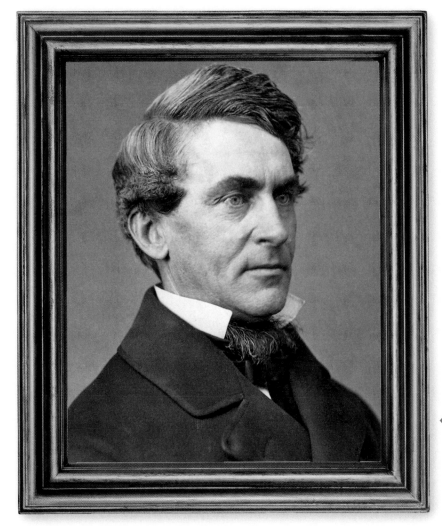

◄ *Arthur appointed Frederick T. Frelinghuysen secretary of state.*

The move angered Conkling and other Stalwarts, but it set the tone for the rest of Arthur's presidency. He had come into office with the reputation of being part of a corrupt political machine. As president, however, Arthur tried to act with the nation's best interest in mind. For example, once Arthur became president, he changed his mind about fixing the way government jobs were awarded. He spoke out strongly in favor of ending the spoils system.

Arthur had the support of many people in this effort to end government corruption. Conkling and other machine politicians resisted, but finally Congress passed the Pendleton Act in January 1883. Named for its author, Ohio senator George Pendleton, the law established a new system for filling federal government jobs. The jobs would be given out based on who was most qualified. Under the law, federal government workers would also have to pass exams to earn job promotions. The Pendleton Act ended the practice of giving out jobs in return for political favors. It dealt a deadly blow to the spoils system.

President Arthur also supported efforts to punish corrupt government officials. The most famous corruption case during Arthur's presidency centered on the Star Route frauds. These incidents involved Post Office officials who

◀ Senator George Pendleton of Ohio wrote a law to establish a fairer system of filling federal government jobs.

cheated the government out of a lot of money. The investigation of these corrupt officials began under Garfield, and when Arthur became president, he insisted that it continue. When two well-known Republican Stalwarts turned out to be involved in the corruption,

This politicial cartoon by Thomas Nast used the image of a lion attacking a fox to show Arthur's efforts to prosecute corrupt government workers involved in the Star Route scandal.

A FABLE—WITH A MODERN APPLICATION.

ONE day the Lion went out in search of some thievish animals that had been making depredations on his domain. On the way he fell in with the Fox, and as the latter acted in a suspicious manner, the Lion accused him of being one of the rascals he was looking for. The Fox, thinking to divert the Lion's attention, protested that he was no worse than others, and hypocritically pleaded that he did not know he had been doing anything wrong. "That is no excuse," said the Lion; "I shall not permit you to escape punishment; and will deal with your confederates also according to their deserts, whenever they fall into my power."

some people criticized Arthur for embarrassing his own party. In fact, much of Arthur's work to make government more honest angered his old Republican friends.

Arthur had to battle members of his own party in Congress over other important issues during his presidency. The biggest clash was over **tariffs.** In the 1880s, U.S. tariffs and taxes were so high that the government had more money than it needed. Arthur believed that lowering the tariffs by a large amount would help the American economy. Republicans in Congress were not so sure. They ignored Arthur and passed a law that lowered tariffs only a little.

▲ *In this 1880s political cartoon, Father Christmas brings many gifts, including a new backbone for President Arthur, a new navy, tariff reductions, and cheap postage.*

Arthur also disagreed with members of Congress over the 1882 Rivers and Harbors Act. The **bill** was intended to improve the nation's waterways. However, Arthur thought that many of the projects covered by

A view of the East ▼ River Harbor in New York City in the mid 1880s

the bill were wasteful and unnecessary. He claimed that the projects would only help make dishonest politicians and their friends rich. Arthur vetoed the bill, refusing to sign it into law. So many members of Congress supported the bill, however, that it was passed again and became law, despite the president's veto.

Arthur vetoed another bill in 1882 that would have stopped Chinese **immigrants** from entering the United States for twenty years. During the 1880s, more than five million people moved to the United States from all over the world. These new arrivals were often treated unfairly and had to live in awful conditions. Many people thought that too many immigrants were entering the United States. They

▲ A view of Chinatown in San Francisco, California, during the late 1800s

criticized Arthur's veto of the bill that would have kept Chinese immigrants out. When Congress changed the bill to bar Chinese immigrants for only ten years, Arthur gave in and signed the bill into law.

President Arthur was committed to improving the U.S. Navy. Beginning with his first message to Congress in 1881, he urged lawmakers to focus on this task. In 1881, navy ships and equipment were old and outdated. The U.S. Navy lagged far behind the navies of many other countries. Arthur argued that the **fleet** could be improved by building fast and powerful steel ships. In 1883, Congress followed Arthur's lead and approved construction of new ships. This began the modernization of the navy that helped make the United States a world power in the early twentieth century. Arthur is credited with being the "Father of the Steel Navy."

Arthur also modernized the White House. The president was famous for his expensive taste in food, clothing, and furniture. It was said that he owned eighty pairs of pants. Unsurprisingly, Arthur was shocked by the shabby condition of the White House when he arrived in Washington, D.C. After becoming president, he ordered that the building be fixed up and modern-

◄ *Two new steel
ships, the USS
Boston and the
USS Atlanta, in
the New York
Navy Yard in the
early 1890s*

ized before he moved in. The old White House furniture was sold and replaced with the best and most
stylish furniture of the time. Arthur hired the famous

New York designer Louis Comfort Tiffany to supervise the work. Elevators and indoor plumbing were added. Arthur's efforts to modernize the White House cost $30,000, which would be equal to about $2 million today.

Tiffany stained ▾ glass screens decorated the White House in the 1880s.

Arthur moved into the White House in December 1881. He brought with him his sister, Mary Arthur McElroy, who served as hostess in place of the late Nell Arthur. As long as Arthur was president, he placed fresh flowers before a portrait of his beloved Nell every day. He also donated money for a stained glass window in Nell's memory at nearby Saint John's Church. He asked that the window be lit at night so he could see it from the White House.

▲ Mary Arthur McElroy served as the White House hostess for her brother.

Arthur's Last Days

★ ★ ★

James G. Blaine ▼ was the Republican presidential candidate in 1884.

Arthur knew his own time was limited. In 1882, he learned that he suffered from a deadly kidney disease. Arthur kept his illness secret. As the presidential election of 1884 approached, Arthur realized that his health would prevent him from running for president again. He also knew that he had little chance of even becoming the Republican candidate. His efforts to eliminate the spoils system had cost him his own party's support. Arthur quietly told his supporters not to

work for his reelection. In 1884, Republicans chose
James G. Blaine to be their candidate for president.
Blaine lost the election to Democrat Grover Cleveland.

    Arthur left the White House on March 4, 1885. He
moved to New York City, and within a year became very
ill. Besides kidney disease, Arthur had developed a serious heart problem. He was too ill to work or to pursue

▼ *Fishing was one
of the president's
favorite pastimes,
but Arthur (left) was
unable to enjoy the
sport once he became
seriously ill.*

favorite pastimes like fishing. He died on November 18, 1886, in New York City. His children, Alan and Nell, were at his side. President Grover Cleveland went to Albany, New York, to pay his respects as Arthur was laid to rest.

Chester Arthur's performance as president surprised the nation. He came into office at a time when politics and government were marked by dishonesty and corruption. Arthur himself was a machine politician who had

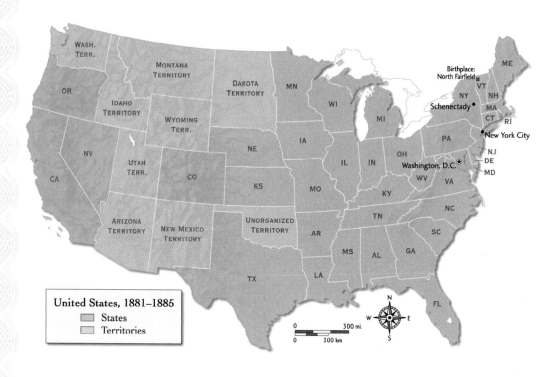

United States, 1881–1885
- States
- Territories

◀ Chester Arthur
spent much of his
presidency trying to
end government
corruption.

been helped by the spoils system. When he became president, most people expected Arthur to fill government offices with his corrupt friends. Instead, he used his power to help clean up government and reduce corruption. His actions cost him the support of his own party.

Arthur was never elected president, but his honest and selfless conduct in that office after the death of James Garfield won him the respect of the nation. After Arthur's death, one newspaper noted, "He earned and deserved the honest fame he possesses."

The tomb of Chester A. Arthur is located near Albany, New York. ▼

GLOSSARY

★ ★ ★

bill—a proposed law

brawl—an often noisy argument

campaigned—participated in an organized effort to win an election

candidate—someone running for office in an election

corrupt—willing to break laws to get money or power

fleet—a country's entire navy or group of warships

immigrants—people who move from one country to live permanently in another

militia—an army of part-time soldiers

pneumonia—a disease of the lungs

tariffs—taxes placed on certain foreign goods entering a country

CHESTER A. ARTHUR'S LIFE AT A GLANCE

★ ★ ★

PERSONAL

Nickname:	The Gentleman Boss, Elegant Arthur
Birth date:	October 5, 1829
Birthplace:	Fairfield, Vermont
Father's name:	William Arthur
Mother's name:	Malvina Stone Arthur
Education:	Graduated from Union College in 1848
Wife's name:	Ellen Lewis Herndon Arthur (1837–1880)
Married:	October 25, 1859
Children:	William Lewis Herndon Arthur (1860–1863), Chester Alan Arthur (1864–1937), Ellen Herndon Arthur (1871–1915)
Died:	November 18, 1886, in New York City
Buried:	Near Albany, New York

PUBLIC

Occupation before presidency:	Lawyer, politician
Occupation after presidency:	Lawyer
Military service:	None
Other government positions:	Collector of the Port of New York; vice president
Political party:	Republican
Vice president:	None
Dates in office:	September 20, 1881–March 3, 1885
Presidential opponents:	Not elected
Number of votes (Electoral College):	Not elected
Selected Writings:	None

Chester A. Arthur's Cabinet

Secretary of state:
James G. Blaine (1881)
Frederick T. Frelinghuysen (1881–1885)

Secretary of the treasury:
William Windom (1881)
Charles J. Folger (1881–1884)
Walter Q. Gresham (1884)
Hugh McCulloch (1884–1885)

Secretary of war:
Robert Todd Lincoln (1881–1885)

Attorney general:
Wayne McVeagh (1881)
Benjamin H. Brewster (1882–1885)

Postmaster general:
Thomas L. James (1881–1882)
Timothy O. Howe (1882–1883)
Walter Q. Gresham (1883–1884)
Frank Hatton (1884–1885)

Secretary of the navy:
William H. Hunt (1881–1882)
William E. Chandler (1882–1885)

Secretary of the interior:
Samuel J. Kirkwood (1881–1882)
Henry M. Teller (1882–1885)

CHESTER A. ARTHUR'S LIFE AND TIMES

★ ★ ★

ARTHUR'S LIFE		WORLD EVENTS	
October 5, Chester Arthur is born in Fairfield, Vermont	1829	1829	The first practical sewing machine is invented by French tailor Barthélemy Thimonnier
	1830		
		1833	Great Britain abolishes slavery
		1836	Texans defeat Mexican troops at San Jacinto after a deadly battle at the Alamo (below)
		1837	American banker J.P. Morgan is born
	1840	1840	Auguste Rodin, famous sculptor of *The Thinker* (right), is born

ARTHUR'S LIFE

1848 Graduates from Union College (below) in Schenectady, New York

Becomes a lawyer **1854**

Starts his own law firm **1856**

1850

WORLD EVENTS

1848 *The Communist Manifesto,* by German writer Karl Marx (right), is widely distributed

1852 American Harriet Beecher Stowe (below) publishes *Uncle Tom's Cabin*

1858 English scientist Charles Darwin (above) presents his theory of evolution

ARTHUR'S LIFE		WORLD EVENTS

Marries Ellen Lewis Herndon — 1859

1860 — 1860 — Austrian composer Gustav Mahler (below) is born in Kalischt (now in Austria)

Becomes the quartermaster general (below) for the New York militia during the Civil War — 1862

1865 — *Tristan and Isolde,* by German composer Richard Wagner, opens in Munich

Lewis Carroll writes *Alice's Adventures in Wonderland*

1868 — Louisa May Alcott publishes *Little Women*

1869 — The periodic table of elements is invented

The transcontinental railroad across the United States is completed (below)

ARTHUR'S LIFE

WORLD EVENTS

1870 John D. Rockefeller founds the Standard Oil Company

Appointed collector   **1871**
of customs for the
Port of New York

1876 The Battle of the Little Bighorn is a victory for Native Americans defending their homes in the West against General George Custer (above)

Alexander Graham Bell uses the first telephone to speak to his assistant, Thomas Watson

1877 German inventor Nikolaus A. Otto works on what will become the internal combustion engine for automobiles

1879 Electric lights are invented

Elected vice   **1880**
president under
James A. Garfield

1870

1880

ARTHUR'S LIFE

July 2, President
James A. Garfield is
shot (below)   1881

September 19,
Garfield dies;
Arthur takes office
early the next day

December 7, moves
into the White House
(below) after having
it modernized

Signs a bill stopping
Chinese immigration
for ten years   1882

WORLD EVENTS

1881   An American
branch of the Red
Cross is founded

First Japanese political
parties are formed

1882   Thomas Edison
(above) builds a
power station

ARTHUR'S LIFE

Signs the Pendleton
Act, named after
George Pendleton
(below), into law,
changing the way
government jobs
are awarded

1883

Resumes his law
practice

1885

November 18, dies in
New York City

1886

WORLD EVENTS

1884

Mark Twain (above)
publishes *The
Adventures of
Huckleberry Finn*

1885

The world's first
skyscraper is built in
Chicago, Illinois

1886

Grover Cleveland
dedicates the Statue of
Liberty in New York

Bombing in
Haymarket Square,
Chicago (below), due
to labor unrest

UNDERSTANDING CHESTER A. ARTHUR AND HIS PRESIDENCY

★ ★ ★

IN THE LIBRARY

Brunelli, Carol. *Chester A. Arthur: Our Twenty-First President.*
Chanhassen, Minn.: The Child's World, 2002.

Joseph, Paul. *Chester Arthur.* Edina, Minn.: Abdo & Daughters, 2000.

Simon, Charnan. *Chester A. Arthur: Twenty-First President
of the United States.* Danbury, Conn.: Children's Press, 1989.

ON THE WEB

The White House—Chester A. Arthur
http://www.whitehouse.gov/history/presidents/ca21.html
For a brief biography of Arthur

Internet Public Library—Chester A. Arthur
http://www.ipl.org/div/potus/caarthur.html
For information about Arthur's presidency
and many links to other resources

The American Presidency—Chester A. Arthur
http://gi.grolier.com/presidents/ea/bios/21parth.html
To read more about Arthur's career

ARTHUR HISTORIC SITES
ACROSS THE COUNTRY

Vermont Division for Historic Preservation
Chester A. Arthur State Historic Site
Route 36
Fairfield, VT 05455
802/828-3051
www.HistoricVermont.org
To see the reconstructed two-room
house where the Arthur family lived

Chester A. Arthur Gravesite
Albany Rural Cemetery
Menands, NY 12204
518/463-7017
To visit the spot where Arthur is buried

THE U.S. PRESIDENTS
(Years in Office)

★ ★ ★

1. **George Washington**
   (March 4, 1789–March 3, 1797)
2. **John Adams**
   (March 4, 1797–March 3, 1801)
3. **Thomas Jefferson**
   (March 4, 1801–March 3, 1809)
4. **James Madison**
   (March 4, 1809–March 3, 1817)
5. **James Monroe**
   (March 4, 1817–March 3, 1825)
6. **John Quincy Adams**
   (March 4, 1825–March 3, 1829)
7. **Andrew Jackson**
   (March 4, 1829–March 3, 1837)
8. **Martin Van Buren**
   (March 4, 1837–March 3, 1841)
9. **William Henry Harrison**
   (March 6, 1841–April 4, 1841)
10. **John Tyler**
    (April 6, 1841–March 3, 1845)
11. **James K. Polk**
    (March 4, 1845–March 3, 1849)
12. **Zachary Taylor**
    (March 5, 1849–July 9, 1850)
13. **Millard Fillmore**
    (July 10, 1850–March 3, 1853)
14. **Franklin Pierce**
    (March 4, 1853–March 3, 1857)
15. **James Buchanan**
    (March 4, 1857–March 3, 1861)
16. **Abraham Lincoln**
    (March 4, 1861–April 15, 1865)
17. **Andrew Johnson**
    (April 15, 1865–March 3, 1869)

18. **Ulysses S. Grant**
    (March 4, 1869–March 3, 1877)
19. **Rutherford B. Hayes**
    (March 4, 1877–March 3, 1881)
20. **James Garfield**
    (March 4, 1881–Sept 19, 1881)
21. **Chester Arthur**
    (Sept 20, 1881–March 3, 1885)
22. **Grover Cleveland**
    (March 4, 1885–March 3, 1889)
23. **Benjamin Harrison**
    (March 4, 1889–March 3, 1893)
24. **Grover Cleveland**
    (March 4, 1893–March 3, 1897)
25. **William McKinley**
    (March 4, 1897–
    September 14, 1901)
26. **Theodore Roosevelt**
    (September 14, 1901–
    March 3, 1909)
27. **William Howard Taft**
    (March 4, 1909–March 3, 1913)
28. **Woodrow Wilson**
    (March 4, 1913–March 3, 1921)
29. **Warren G. Harding**
    (March 4, 1921–August 2, 1923)
30. **Calvin Coolidge**
    (August 3, 1923–March 3, 1929)
31. **Herbert Hoover**
    (March 4, 1929–March 3, 1933)
32. **Franklin D. Roosevelt**
    (March 4, 1933–April 12, 1945)

33. **Harry S. Truman**
    (April 12, 1945–
    January 20, 1953)
34. **Dwight D. Eisenhower**
    (January 20, 1953–
    January 20, 1961)
35. **John F. Kennedy**
    (January 20, 1961–
    November 22, 1963)
36. **Lyndon B. Johnson**
    (November 22, 1963–
    January 20, 1969)
37. **Richard M. Nixon**
    (January 20, 1969–
    August 9, 1974)
38. **Gerald R. Ford**
    (August 9, 1974–
    January 20, 1977)
39. **James Earl Carter**
    (January 20, 1977–
    January 20, 1981)
40. **Ronald Reagan**
    (January 20, 1981–
    January 20, 1989)
41. **George H. W. Bush**
    (January 20, 1989–
    January 20, 1993)
42. **William Jefferson Clinton**
    (January 20, 1993–
    January 20, 2001)
43. **George W. Bush**
    (January 20, 2001–)

INDEX

★ ★ ★

ABOUT THE AUTHOR

Andrew Santella writes for magazines and newspapers, including *GQ* and the *New York Times Book Review*. He is the author of a number of books for young readers. He lives outside Chicago, with his wife and son.